Hello Everyone,

My Name is **Mohit Badaya**

Welcome to www.mohittech2.blogspot.com e-book,

From a Small Child to a Aged Person This E-Book is fun and favorable for people of all People Groups.

People Search Here and there for finding best apps to download or best games to download and play on their smart phones, but unfortunately they get confused by seeing so inappropriate and less knowledgeable manner and get distress. So, Built up For You People , Helping Everyone For getting #**Useful ,Beautiful, Helping, Best, Educational, Adventurous, Communication** and also so many other categorized apps available for FREE. These Applications Are Just like Your Friend, They Can help you in need, Solve Your problems, Make You aware, and also make you updated with Latest Information and all the latest updates in the world. These Applications are User Friendly And Easily available for FREE on Play Store, So need not to worry & just Hang on and be Cool………..

You Can Also go to http://www.mohittech2.blogspot.com for some cool tips and updates with latest Gadget Reviews for FREE…

1. GOOGLE TRANSLATE

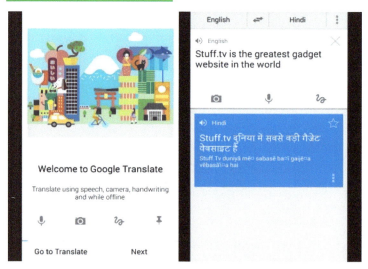

We've seen a few clever translation apps in our time, but recently Google Translate has crushed them all. It now offers (sometimes clunky, word-for-word) translations of over 70 languages with input via text, handwritten words or symbols, spoken words or even text recognition via the camera. It can then give you the translation in the form of text or speak it for you.

The core app can do all this with a data connection, and language packs can be downloaded for free so you can use it abroad without the need for Wi-Fi or the fear of roaming data charges.

2. NASA APP

This isn't the best looking app in the world, but it's full of geek-level info and media from the NASA archive, along with news and updates on what's going on up there and back at base. Maybe one day they'll get a slick front end for it all, but for now this raggle-taggle collection of links, pictures, videos and news feeds has plenty to keep space cadets informed and entertained.

3. TWICKETS

Twickets is a way to buy or sell spare tickets to gigs or events, but what makes it special is the rule that tickets can only change hands for their face value or less. That means the profiteering touts stay away and genuine fans get to recyle spares in good faith - great if one of your mates has dropped out and left you in the lurch, or you need an extra seat at short notice.

You can browse what's available or offer tickets via the app and finalise the deal via Twitter (hence the name).

4. AUDIBLE FOR ANDROID

 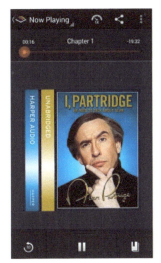

Long journey? Tired eyes? Audio books! A bit like radio shows that you actually want to listen to, a bit like podcasts before all the funny people stopped doing them, a bit like books being read to you (OK, mostly the latter), audio books are a treat to be savoured.

Amazon's Audible app is a gateway to its own audio book service, drawing you in with free tasters of some of its best sellers. It's worth downloading even if it's only for those free nibbles.

5. NAVFREE

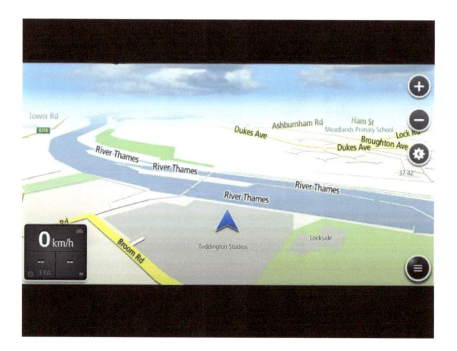

You've got Google Maps already and that's lovely. However, that relies on a data connection, which isn't always available even in your home nation and will sting you with ludicrous charges abroad. Navfree is based on an open-source map database and provides mapping and voice-guided sat-nav for no cash at all.

You can load it with paid extras if you like, but it's fine as it is. Download the local variant for any country you're visiting before you leave and you'll always have a map and a sat-nav tool at your hip.

6. AIRBNB

Hotels are great when other people are paying, or if you have pots of cash to waste, but otherwise they're rarely situated where you want them. Airbnb is one of the stars of the so-called shareconomy, an accommodation network built around normal people offering up their unused rooms for a little bit of extra cash.

The result? You'll be able to find somewhere to stay right in the heart of the city, up a mountain or even down a river, often for a very decent price. Just spend a minute browsing the amazing pads on offer and you'll be hooked.

7. ANY.DO TO-DO LIST & TASK LIST

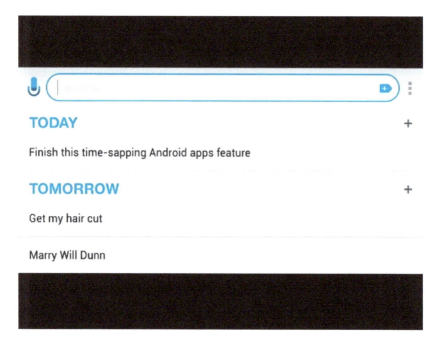

We're all busy. Busy creating Stuff To Do lists and sticking them in our bags, on the front door, in our back pockets and tapping them into note apps on our phones. Any.do is the best way to keep on top of all those loose ends, thanks to its cloud syncing and sharing skills. You can have it running as a live widget on your homescreen and also separate your tasks into different folders.

8. COMICS

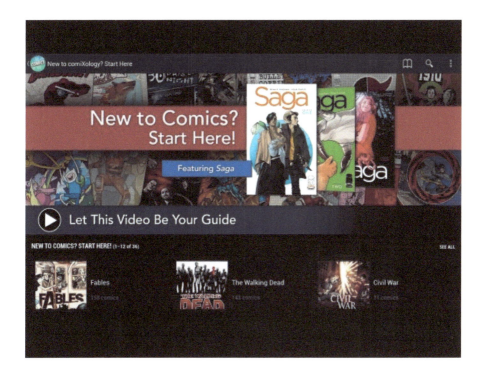

With access to over 45,000 comics from DC, Marvel, Image Comics, IDW and Disney, the Comics app is the place to go for all things graphically novel. You get quite a few freebies to get you started, with more free titles released each week. Paid-for comics will typically set you back between £0.69 and £2.49. The app really comes alive on larger devices, where you can pore over the panels in a more leisurely manner than on a phone.

9. ZOOPLA PROPERTY SEARCH

It won't necessarily find everything in your chosen area, but Zoopla (which incorporated Findaproperty.com in 2012) has a huge amount of properties for sale, and even if it's just used as a jumping off point it can give you a good idea of what's available and the prices involved. The app itself could be easier to use, but it does the basics of allowing you to search on specific area, property type, number of bedrooms and add keywords, then browse photos and link up with the agent.

10. COCKTAIL FLOW - DRINK RECIPES

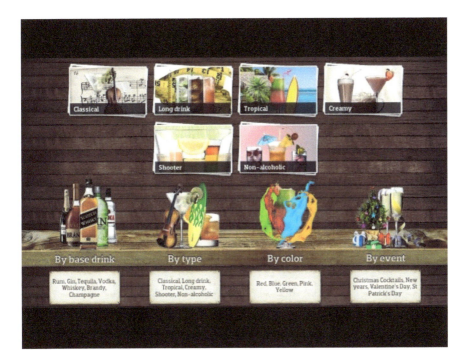

The best feature of this cocktail recipe book is the way you can tell it what odds and ends you've got lurking in the cupboard under the sink, and then ask it to suggest palatable ways to mix them up. It also comes with a library of popular cocktails, with additional packs that can be downloaded for a small fee.

11. MONEY TRACKER

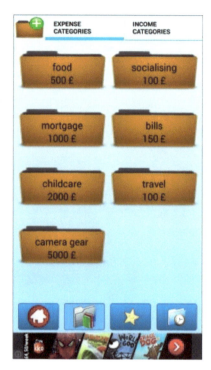

Easily our favourite app for keeping a handle on incomings and outgoings, Money Tracker strikes a sensible balance between simplicity and features. As well as the basic sums, it lets you create your own folders and categories, so you can see where it all goes each month, and more easily define where you might be able to make savings in future. Did you really spend that much on coffee this week? Maybe you should invest in a flask this weekend.

12. HANGOUTS

"Hey! Who wants brunch at Choochies today?" "Count me in! I've got tickets to the Nicks game, wanna come too?" Etc. Alternatively you can use Hangouts to message friends via text, video and emoticon-style "emojis" in a more realistic manner. "Train cancelled again", or "Dad, get on the video call so you can show me how to fix the boiler". That sort of thing. Woah! Hangouts rocks!

13. DUOLINGO: LEARN LANGUAGES FREE

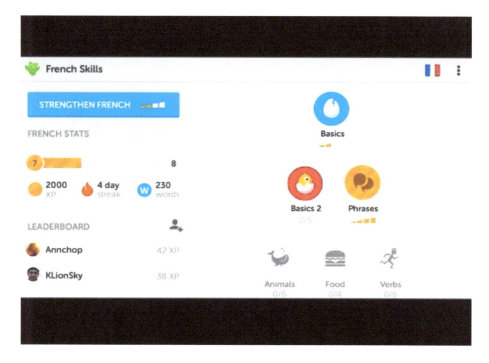

Google Translate may be great, but the long-term aim should be to learn to speak all those languages yourself. Duolingo does an amazing job of making this fun, with a format that's a bit like a pub quiz machine. It currently supports Spanish, French, German, Portuguese, Italian and English, and if you "play" it regularly you'll definitely pick up at least some competence in your chosen language. With more intensive use you can give yourself a week's crash course before a trip abroad.

14. HOUZZ INTERIOR DESIGN IDEAS

This one is all about inspiration. As you would hope from an app about design, Houzz itself is neat, logically laid out, smart and pretty in all the right places, making it the perfect distraction as you recline on your Eames lounge chair, feet up on the ottoman, contemplating the witty juxtaposition of that chandelier in your bedsit.

15. FXGURU: MOVIE FX DIRECTOR

This slightly gimmicky special effects app is nonetheless very clever, verging on useful. It comes with a batch of free effects (the kind of things you'd see in a disaster movie) with additional packs as in-app purchases.

You point your phone or tablet at a scene (say, your office, the street or your garden), and then the app records a short video clip with a destructive missile attack or perhaps a hovering UFO superimposed over the live action. Motion tracking allows you to pan as you film, too.

16. BBC CBEEBIES PLAYTIME

A lot of free apps for children are beset by confusing prompts for in-app purchases that can seriously hamper the fun. CBeebies Playtime is an ad-free lucky dip of educational games and activities for pre-school children, based on some of the channel's biggest shows and characters, including Mr Tumble, Tree Fu Tom, The Octanauts and real-life actual people such as Andy and Nina.

17. SOUNDCLOUD

SoundCloud is great because it's not just the same old music rehashed in a new, futile money-making shell. It does hold a lot of full-length commercial tracks but it's the unique user-generated music that makes it special. That means DJ mixes, remixes, cover versions, live recordings and recitals, snippets, sounds and spoken word contibutions. If you want to listen beyond the sphere of Spotify, cock your ear this way.

18. MET OFFICE WEATHER APPLICATION

All UK weather forecasts are based on information and predictions from the Met Office, so why not get your forecast from the horse's mouth? This app doesn't go in for swanky visuals but does give it to you straight, with timeline breakdowns of the changing skies plus map-based predictions of advancing weather systems. If you're less of a weather geek, try the BBC Weather app for a prettier presentation of much the same stuff.

19. VLC FOR ANDROID BETA

Wouldn't it be lovely if there was one video format to rule them all, like MP3 is to music? Well, dream on... Until that day you'll be thankful for VLC, which aims to play every video format you'll ever encounter. If you like to source your movies from varied locations you'll find this one of the most useful apps on your phone or tablet. It's ad-free and doesn't try to harvest all your personal data either, which makes a nice change.

20. DROPBOX

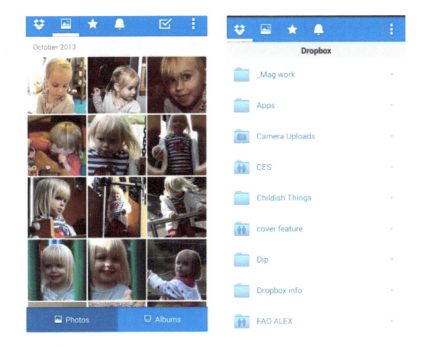

As Android moves closer to home computer territory, syncing photos, music and work documents is increasingly important. As a free service, Dropbox offers 2GB of pleasingly simple online storage which is automatically synced whenever you log in from any of your devices – very useful for occassional file transfers, semi-permanent documents and shared folders. The Android app is nothing fancy but it doesn't need to be, getting the job done without fuss.

21. RUNKEEPER - GPS TRACK RUN WALK

If you're putting yourself through a fitness grind alone, this virtual back-patter will help spur you on. It tracks all your runs, walks and rides, then does the maths to tell you (and the entire world via social media) how many calories you've burnt, how far you've gone and generally how heroic you've been over the past week or so. The in-app purchase model keeps it all nice and tidy too, so even in the basic free format it's a very neat app to use.

22. WIFI FILE TRANSFER

Google's liberal management of the Play store leads to some strange situations, such as the presence of six apps with exactly the same name. Here we're referring to the one developed by smarterDroid. We find it the easiest way to move files wirelessly to and from a computer and an Android device on an ad-hoc basis. The free version has a file size limit of 5MB, but you can buy the full, unlimited version for £0.88.

23. PEPPA'S PAINTBOX

We don't review childen's cartoons, but if we did, Peppa Pig would get five stars because it's consistently brilliant in its own little way, full of practical education wrapped up in addictively snappy episodes. Like the CBeebies app, this porcine painting app has no hidden agenda so your kids can paint away without being tripped up or led astray by ads, links or in-app purchases. Madame Gazelle would certainly approve.

24. TUNEIN RADIO

Take a break from the endless banality of UK radio and tune in to a different point of view or musical selection. So long as you have a half-decent data connection, this app will tickle your ears with audio streams from all over the world, browsable by location, genre or what's trending. It also works as an on-demand podcast player. It's brilliant for in-car entertainment, so long as you have a data contract that can take the strain.

25. VINE

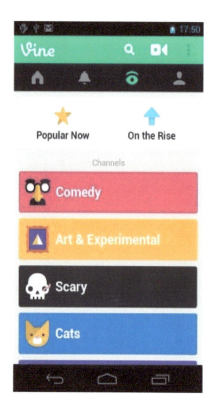 

One of the best ways to get your fix of LOLs is to flick your way through Vine's stream of micro-movies. The quality is always going to vary, but the way the app delivers them is beautifully quick and simple. Just check out your feed or do a search (say, #skatefails), then enjoy a string of LOLable 4-second loops. Maybe even upload a few of your own.

26. POCKET

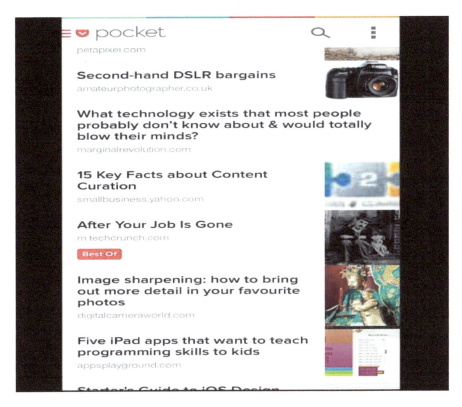

An absolutely indispensable app, Pocket lets you save webpages for offline reading. It's super-easy to use, installing a shortcut into your mobile browser so you can send articles over to it with a click; extensions for desktop browsers are also available, so if something catches your eye at work you can whisk it over to the app for reading on the commute home.

Once in the app you can easily share articles with other people or to social media and it'll even strip out ads from the articles if you want it to. Frankly, we can't imagine life without it.

27. FEEDLY

With the demise of Google Reader, the world needed an alternative RSS reader - and Feedly fits the bill nicely.

It does pretty much everything you'd want an RSS reader to do, presenting the latest stories from your favourite media outlets and blogs in an attractive, easily browsable list. You'll find every site you might ever be interested in - yes, Stuff.tv is in there - plus it integrates neatly with the likes of Pocket and Evernote and sharing stories to social media is but a matter of a click.

28. FLIPBOARD

The basic idea behind Flipboard is that turns your social media feeds into a constantly updating magazine, displaying the latest updates from Twitter, Facebook, Google+, Instagram and many more in a lovely grid-based design. But there's a lot more to it than that, with the ability to add content from specific RSS feeds or just by subject making it a truly personalised digital mag.

It's ridiculously simple to use and works so well that Samsung used it to power its My Magazine app for its latest smartphones. High praise indeed.

29. LOKLOK

Now here's an interesting idea: an editable lockscreen that you use to share pictures and notes with your friends. Confused? So were we to start with.

Basically, you set a picture as your lockscreen then scribble on top of it. Whatever you draw or write will then appear on top of the lockscreens of all those in your LokLok group.

The app is (presumably) intended to be used for swiftly sharing notes and pics between people, without them even having to unlock their phone. But of course we used it to share juvenile scrawlings with each other. Ahem.

It's currently in beta, so expect a few bugs, but hopefully they'll be ironed out soon.

30. ROUTESHOOT VIDEO AND GPS APP

Like a blend of GoPro, Strava and Google Streetview, RouteShoot lets healthy types create map-based videos of their latest adventures then share them for route guidance, improving technique or simply entertainment.

You'll need a smartphone mount to get the most out of it - certainly if you plan to use it on your bike - but once that's sorted it'll use your phone's camera to shoot footage of your latest off-road excursion, linking it with a map of where you've been and providing data on elevation and speed. An in-app purchase adds HD video, but really the quality of the footage is less important here than the ability to share routes with your mates.

31.AMAZON

* Customers are able to shop any of Amazon's sites around the world from a single app
* Quickly search, get product details, and read reviews on millions of products from Amazon and other merchants
* Take advantage of 1-Click ordering, customer support, Wish Lists, order tracking, and more
* Compare prices and check availability instantly by scanning a barcode, using Flow, or typing your search
* Check out Gold Box Deals - including the Deal of the Day and Lightning Deals, and get deal push notifications
* Send and share links to products via email, SMS, Facebook, Twitter, and more
* Shop the full selection of products available at Amazon.com
* Buy with confidence, knowing that all transactions are securely processed

Product Description

The Amazon app lets you shop and manage your Amazon orders from anywhere. Browse and shop by department, compare prices, read reviews, share products with friends, check out Gold Box Deals, make purchases, and check the status of your orders.

Check prices and availability by scanning a barcode, using Flow, or typing your search. You can also stay on top of Lightning Deals, the Deal of the Day, and ship and delivery confirmations with push notifications.

With the Amazon App, you always have full access to your Shopping Cart, Wish Lists, payment and Prime shipping options, Subscribe & Save order history, and 1-Click settings, just like on the full Amazon.com site.

32.Fast & Furious Game

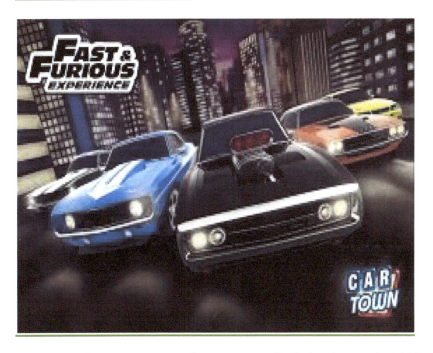

*** Show off your summer style! Get 30% off all visual upgrades! ***

Step into the world of Fast & Furious 6. Join the Fast & Furious crew as they prepare to take on a series of jobs in an all new heist mode. Earn cash and the respect of the "Fastest" drivers as you drift and drag through the London street racing scene and take on opponents in Race Wars events.

Fast & Furious 6: The Game takes mobile racing to new heights with stunning graphics, new game modes, addictive online races and exciting full throttle missions.

JOIN THE FAST & FURIOUS 6 CREW
Take down a crew of lethally skilled mercenary drivers to earn respect as you drift and drag through the streets of London.

SHOW OFF YOUR STYLE
Collect, customize and upgrade a variety of high end licensed cars including hero cars from the movie Fast & Furious 6 - all featuring stunning graphics.

PULL OFF ONE LAST JOB
Earn gold and coins by pulling thrilling heists with the Fast & Furious 6 crew and hero cars.

COMPETE
Rule tournaments, race online, or join a crew and take on the world by dominating the global leaderboards.

And Hereby I end Up All the Amazing and Most valued FREE apps on Android Store

So, How You Liked Our First E-Book. Hope It is Good and You liked it very much.

You Can also go to http://www.mohittech2.blogspot.com for latest updates and latest technology related things.

If any Suggestions, Questions, Or Any other type Of queries related to this E-Book or any matter on Technology

Feel Free To Contact me at:-

Website:- http://www.mohittech2.blogspot.com

E-Mail:- mohit.bad1997@gmail.com

Facebook:- https://www.facebook.com/pages/Tech-Darbaar/1506618266223178?ref=hl

Thank You For Reading……..

www.ingramcontent.com/pod-product-compliance
Lightning Source LLC
Chambersburg PA
CBHW041148050326
40689CB00001B/526